REDUCING POLLUTION AND WASTE

Jen Green

Chicago, Illinois

www.heinemannraintree.com
Visit our website to find out more information about Heinemann-Raintree books.

To order:
☎ Phone 888-454-2279
💻 Visit www.heinemannraintree.com to browse our catalog and order online.

© 2012 Raintree
an imprint of Capstone Global Library, LLC
Chicago, Illinois

Visit our website at www.heinemannraintree.com

All rights reserved. No part of this publication may be reproduced or transmitted in any form or by any means, electronic or mechanical, including photocopying, recording, taping, or any information storage and retrieval system, without permission in writing from the publisher.

Edited by Andrew Farrow and Adrian Vigliano
Designed by Victoria Allen
Original illustrations © Capstone Global Library Ltd.
Illustrated by Tower Designs UK Limited
Picture research by Mica Brancic
Production by Eirian Griffiths
Originated by Capstone Global Library Ltd.
Printed and bound in the United States of America by Corporate Graphics in North Mankato, Minnesota.

15 14 13 12 11
10 9 8 7 6 5 4 3 2 1

Library of Congress Cataloging-in-Publication Data
Cataloging-in-Publication data is on file at the Library of Congress.

ISBNs:
978-1-4109-4320-0 (HC)
978-1-4109-4327-9 (PB)

Acknowledgments
The author and publishers are grateful to the following for permission to reproduce copyright material: Corbis p. 13 Photolibrary/Monsoon/© Allen Russell p. 14 © Reuters, p. 15 © Julie Dermansky, p. 16 © Roger Ressmeyer, p. 21 Reuters/© HO, p. 25 © Ryan Pyle, p. 26 © Ed Kashi, p. 30 © Paul Souders, p. 34 © Radius Images; Getty Images p. 4 Bloomberg/Arni Saeberg, p. 5 Matt Cardy, p. 6 Susan Schulman, p. 7 Science Faction/Karen Kasmauski, p. 9 Christopher Furlong, p. 17 AFP Photo/Belga/Olivier Matthys, p. 18 AFP Photo/Neil Jones, p. 23 Iconica/Nico Kai, p. 24 AFP Photo/Indranil Mukherjee, p. 27 AFP Photo, p. 28 isifa/Libor Fojtik, p. 31 Science & Society Picture Library, p. 33 Steffen Kugler, p. 35 AFP Photo/Manan Vatsyayana, p. 36 Blend Images/Ariel Skelley, p. 38 Wathiq Khuzaie, p. 39 AFP Photo/Dibyangshu Sarkar, p. 40 Taxi/Steve Ryan; Reuters p. 37; Shutterstock p. 11 © Ssuaphotos.

Cover photograph of boys looking for scrap metal in Manila's largest landfill used with permission of Getty Images/David Greedy.

We would like to thank Michael D. Mastrandrea, Ph.D., for his invaluable help in the preparation of this book.

Every effort has been made to contact copyright holders of any material reproduced in this book. Any omissions will be rectified in subsequent printings if notice is given to the publisher.

Disclaimer
All the Internet addresses (URLs) given in this book were valid at the time of going to press. However, due to the dynamic nature of the Internet, some addresses may have changed, or sites may have changed or ceased to exist since publication. While the author and publisher regret any inconvenience this may cause readers, no responsibility for any such changes can be accepted by either the author or the publisher.

Contents

Polluted Earth..4

Where Do Pollution and Waste Come From?..6

The Impact of Pollution and Waste...12

Local and Global Pollution 18

Who Produces Pollution and Waste? 22

Tackling Pollution 28

Reduce, Reuse, and Recycle 36

Facts and Figures...42

Glossary..44

Find Out More..46

Index..48

Words appearing in the text in bold, **like this**, are explained in the glossary.

Polluted Earth

When the natural world is harmed by waste, or by any substance that does not belong there, we call it **pollution**. Around the world, pollution and waste are building up. They are threatening Earth.

What is pollution?

Pollution damages the air, water, and soil. Some pollution occurs naturally. For example, erupting volcanoes can **pollute**, or dirty, the **environment** (our natural surroundings). But most pollution is caused by humans. For example, dirty water spilling into a river is a common form of pollution.

In 2010 a volcano erupted in Iceland. This was a natural form of pollution.

People sometimes leave piles of garbage on the street or in the countryside. This is wasteful. It can also cause pollution.

The environment challenge

Pollution and waste are now threatening the well-being of our planet. People in wealthy countries like the United States use more of Earth's **natural resources**— such as water and oil—than they need. They also create huge amounts of waste.

This way of life is not **sustainable**. It cannot go on forever. People are using up Earth's resources faster than they can be replaced.

This book will explore the problems of pollution and waste. It will ask you to take the environment challenge. Look closely at the issues. Then decide what the best solutions are—for you and for the world.

Looking for evidence

This book contains suggestions for carrying out your own research. You can use many different sources. Library books are a good source. So are newspapers and television reports. The Internet is a useful source of information. But not all websites are reliable. Try government websites and organizations with addresses ending in ".gov" or ".org." When researching facts, try to find two separate sources.

WORD BANK

environment   natural world surrounding us on Earth
pollute   when harmful substances dirty the air, water, or soil
pollution   when the natural world is harmed by waste or by any substance that does not belong there
sustainable   when resources are managed so that they will not run out in the future

Where Do Pollution and Waste Come From?

As the number of people on Earth increases, so do levels of **pollution** and waste.

Industry and manufacturing

Serious pollution began in the early 1800s. During this period, people in Europe and North America began burning coal. They did so to create power for machinery. But this produced smoke and a black, powdery material called **soot**. As more countries developed **industries** (business that make things), pollution increased. Some industries today produce poisonous waste.

Farming

Farming also causes pollution. Most modern farmers use harmful substances to increase plant growth. They spray crops with other harmful substances to kill weeds and insects. These substances kill living things in the soil. They can also leak into nearby rivers.

Mining (digging for valuable materials) causes serious pollution. Miners in South America often use a substance called mercury. Mercury poisons life in the river.

Hunger for energy

Creating power, or **energy**, is another major cause of pollution. Substances like coal and oil are known as **fossil fuels**. They are the world's main energy source. But burning fossil fuels produces pollution. This is seriously harming the **environment** (see page 20).

Nuclear energy is another energy source. It is made by working with a metal called uranium. Nuclear energy does not produce air pollution. But it does produce waste that is **radioactive**. This means it gives off tiny **rays** (lines or beams) of harmful energy. The waste remains harmful for thousands of years. It is stored in sealed containers, usually underground.

Workers must keep track of radioactive waste. They need to wear protective suits.

WORD BANK

fossil fuel   fuel, such as coal, oil, and natural gas, that is made of the remains of plants or animals that lived millions of years ago

industry   type of work that creates something to be sold

nuclear energy   form of energy that is made by using a metal called uranium

radioactive   something that gives off harmful rays, or beams, of energy

Domestic waste

Household waste presents a huge problem. In the United States, a family of four throws away about 2,700 kilograms (6,000 pounds) of garbage each year.

Waste produced by cities, towns, and other settled areas is called **municipal solid waste (MSW)**. This includes garbage from stores, offices, restaurants, schools, hospitals, and homes. MSW includes large amounts of food scraps. It also includes huge amounts of paper, glass, plastic, clothing, and old machinery.

Problem packaging

The contents of the average garbage can includes huge amounts of packaging. These are the wrappings that contain the food and other goods we buy from stores and supermarkets. This presents a huge waste of **natural resources**, **energy**, and money.

This pie chart shows the amounts of different materials thrown away. It represents a typical household in a country like the United States.

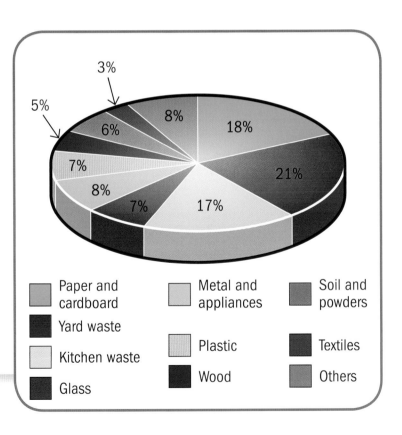

Legend:
- Paper and cardboard
- Yard waste
- Kitchen waste
- Glass
- Metal and appliances
- Plastic
- Wood
- Soil and powders
- Textiles
- Others

Waste collection

In many countries, local governments make sure garbage is collected from people's homes. Governments then spend huge amounts of money disposing of MSW safely. Some governments also collect items that can be **recycled**, or turned into other products.

Some local governments collect materials for recycling at the curbside. Others provide special recycling centers.

WORD BANK
municipal solid waste (MSW)   waste produced by cities, towns, and other settled areas
natural resource   something useful that is provided by nature
recycle   save garbage so it can be turned into another product

Will it rot?

One hundred years ago, most waste was made up of **organic** (natural) materials. These included paper, wood, wool, and cloth. These materials **biodegrade**, or rot away, quickly in nature.

Today, garbage contains a lot of **synthetic** (human-made) materials. These include plastics, glass, and ceramics like flowerpots. These materials take a long time to biodegrade. Some never break down.

Find out more

Investigate the materials used in the packaging found in your home. Paper, cardboard, glass, and aluminum are commonly used in packaging. So are plastics such as foam. Use the table at right to figure out how long each material you find will take to rot away.

Time to rot away	Name of object
2–4 weeks	Paper
1–3 months	Leaves
6 months	Fruit peel
5 years	Drink carton
10+ years	Plastic bags
50+ years	Plastic food container
80 years	Aluminum can
100 years	Tin can
400+ years	Plastic bottle
500+ years	Glass bottle
Never	Many foam plastics

The table shows the time it takes for organic and synthetic materials to rot.

Everyday energy

As we have read, **energy** use is a source of **pollution**. This is because the burning of **fossil fuels** such as coal produces pollution. We use energy every time we switch on a light, watch television, or use a computer.

We can also cause pollution when we travel. Cars, buses, trains, and planes run on fossil fuels such as gasoline. As these fuels burn, they give off harmful waste **gases**. (A gas is a substance without a definite shape, like air.) Traveling by car produces far more pollution per person than using buses or trains.

Harmful waste

Paints, weed killers, bleach, and detergent all contain harmful substances. These should be thrown away carefully. **Sewage** (dirty water) can also cause health problems. In wealthy countries like the United States, wastewater containing sewage is usually treated, or cleaned. This makes it safe to return to rivers and streams. But this is often not the case in poorer countries.

Vehicles are a major cause of pollution in cities and near highways.

WORD BANK
biodegrade   rot away naturally
organic   made from natural materials
sewage   dirty water from homes that contains harmful substances and waste
synthetic   made by humans, not nature

The Impact of Pollution and Waste

Pollution can enter the air, water, or soil. The wind or water then help to spread **pollutants** (polluting substances) further.

Chain of life

Once in the **environment**, pollutants harm living things. Plants, animals, and people take in the pollutants. All living things are part of a **food chain**. In a food chain, larger living things eat smaller living things. Tiny living things near the bottom of the chain commonly take in pollutants. The pollutants are then passed on to the larger creatures that eat the smaller ones. These larger creatures include eagles, sharks, polar bears— and humans.

Harmful substances used in farming are taken in by insects. They then pass up the food chain to large birds such as hawks and owls.

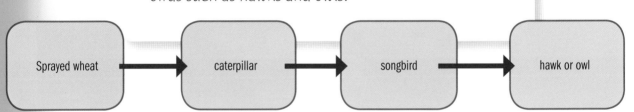

| Sprayed wheat | caterpillar | songbird | hawk or owl |

Air pollution

In many parts of the world, the air contains many pollutants. Factories, **power stations** (places where power is created), and cars are some of the main sources of pollution.

Smog is a form of air pollution that affects many cities. This poisonous air forms when waste **gases** from vehicles react with sunlight. The dirty air can trigger breathing problems in people. Many cities are trying to tackle smog. For example, they are reducing car use in city centers.

World's smoggiest city

Mexico City is the capital of Mexico. It is one of the world's most **polluted** cities. When pollution reaches dangerous levels, school and factory hours are changed. This avoids exposing people to the worst pollution.

Recently, the city has been making a big effort to improve air quality. Vehicles are tested every six months. This keeps the harmful gases cars give off within safe levels. City laws require motorists to leave their cars at home one day a week. They must use public transportation instead.

Pollution levels are often very high in Mexico City.

WORD BANK

food chain way of describing how living things eat other living things from the level below them

pollutant substance that harms the air, water, or land

smog poisonous, dirty air that forms when polluting gases react with sunlight

River pollution

Plants, animals, and people depend on freshwater for survival. But water is often **polluted**. Harmful substances from farmland can pollute rivers. So can **sewage** from cities and factories. This harms fish and other water creatures. People can also get sick from drinking polluted water.

Tainted oceans

Most **pollutants** dumped in rivers end up flowing into the ocean. People also sometimes use the deep waters out at sea to dump garbage. Sometimes this includes poisonous substances and **radioactive** waste. Scientists have discovered that even small amounts of this poisonous **pollution** can damage the oceans' **food chains**.

Oil companies often dig for oil at the bottom of the sea. If something goes wrong with the drilling process, this can lead to oil spills. These are major disasters for the **environment** (see the box at right). Everyday problems like cracked pipes also cause damage over time.

In January 2000, a deadly poison called cyanide leaked from a Romanian gold **mine** into the Tisza River, in eastern Europe. It killed wildlife as far as 400 kilometers (250 miles) downriver.

The Gulf oil spill

In April 2010, a major oil spill occurred in the Gulf of Mexico. The oil company British Petroleum (BP) was digging for oil off the state of Louisiana's coast. There was an explosion on its deep-water **oil rig**. (Oil rigs are special equipment used to drill an oil well.) The explosion killed 11 workers. After the explosion, oil began to gush from the damaged well into the seabed.

By June the spill was rated the worst in the history of the United States. In mid-July, BP managed to cap the well. But by then the oil had polluted hundreds of miles of coastline. It remains to be seen just how badly local food chains will be affected.

A worker sucks spilled oil from the Gulf of Mexico in August 2010. The total bill for the damage may be as high as $20 billion.

WORD BANK
oil rig   special equipment used for drilling an oil well

Pollution and waste in the soil

Soil is an important **natural resource**. Plants need soil to grow. And humans need plants, because plants provide our food. But soil can be **polluted** by **industry**, **mining**, and farming. It can also be polluted by household waste.

In many **developing countries** (poorer countries), garbage is dumped in open areas. Major cities such as Lagos, in Nigeria, and Manila, in the Philippines, are surrounded by huge heaps of rotting waste. This waste attract rats and flies. It can cause disease.

Landfills

In wealthier countries, called **developed countries**, most household waste ends up in pits called **landfills**. Landfill sites present two main **pollution** risks. If the pit is not properly sealed, dirty water can leak into the surrounding soil or water. Also, rotting garbage produces **methane gas**. This can explode if it is not handled safely.

Disposing of our garbage is a major problem worldwide. Many countries are running out of space to build landfill sites.

Recycling

Recycling will play an increasingly important role in waste disposal. Recycling materials such as glass, paper, and aluminum cans saves natural resources. It also reduces **energy** use and cuts waste. But recycling centers are expensive to build and operate. Also, not all materials are easy to recycle (see page 38).

What would YOU do?

Imagine you work for a local government. Existing landfill sites in your area are full. You need to recommend the best way forward. Would you order a study to find new landfill sites? Would you look into burning trash (**incineration**)? Or would you spend money on new recycling centers?

Incineration is the burning of trash. It is an effective means of waste disposal. But few people want it done near their homes, for fear of pollution.

WORD BANK
developed country   wealthy country where many people live comfortably
developing country   country where many people do not live comfortably
landfill   large pit where garbage is packed down and covered with soil
methane   gas produced by rotting garbage

Local and Global Pollution

Pollution is sometimes a local problem. But it can also be a problem that affects many countries.

Passive smoking

Cigarette smoke is an example of harmful local pollution. Tobacco smoke contains dangerous substances that are linked to many illnesses, such as cancer, lung infections, and heart disease. These **pollutants** affect the smoker. But they can also seriously affect other people in the same area. Luckily, smoking is now banned in public places in many countries.

Transboundary pollution

Pollution in the air or water can travel huge distances. When it crosses the borders of different countries, it is called **transboundary pollution**.

Acid rain is an example of transboundary pollution. Acid rain forms when **gases** from cars and factories mix with water in the air. This moisture may drift hundreds of miles, before it falls as rain or snow. Acid rain is then taken in by tree roots and leaves. This can cause whole forests to die. It may also enter lakes and rivers. It can then poison fish.

Cigarette smoke does not just affect the smoker. It also affects other people nearby.

The Chernobyl disaster

Nuclear reactors are places where **nuclear energy** is created. In the mid-1980s, hundreds of nuclear reactors were providing **energy** in the United States, parts of Europe, and Japan. But in 1986 a nuclear reactor at Chernobyl, in the country of Ukraine, caught fire and exploded. An enormous cloud of **radiation** drifted on the wind over much of Europe. When rain fell in some areas, land was **polluted**. Crops and the milk and meat from animals that had eaten the crops had to be destroyed.

Following this disaster, many countries gave up on nuclear energy. But in the early 2000s, nuclear energy again became attractive to governments. This was because of a new awareness of the dangers of burning **fossil fuels**.

People living as far as 330 kilometers (200 miles) from Chernobyl had to leave their homes after the disaster. Scientists think that 10,000 people in the area have now died of illnesses caused by radiation.

WORD BANK

acid rain   rain that has the harmful substance acid in it because of air pollution
nuclear reactor   place where nuclear energy is created
transboundary pollution   pollution that crosses borders between countries

Greenhouse gases

The **atmosphere** is a layer of **gases** that surrounds Earth. Certain gases naturally occur in the atmosphere. These gases are called **greenhouse gases**. They include **carbon dioxide** and **methane** gases. They trap some of the Sun's heat. This helps to produce temperatures that support living things on Earth.

Global warming

Scientists believe that increased levels of greenhouse gases are causing Earth to heat up even more. This effect is called **global warming**. Nearly all scientists are convinced that air **pollution** is causing this temperature rise. For example, we have been adding increasing amounts of carbon dioxide to the atmosphere. This is because burning **fossil fuels** releases carbon dioxide. Carbon dioxide is also released when we cut down forests. Meanwhile, farming practices, such as growing rice and raising cattle, are releasing methane gas.

Feeling the heat

Since 1900 world temperatures have risen by 0.6 °C (1 °F). In cold areas like Antarctica, they have risen even faster. The ice there has started to melt. This water adds to the total amount of water in the oceans.

If levels of greenhouse gases continue to rise, global warming could increase. Rising sea levels could threaten low-lying countries and islands. Much of countries like Egypt, and whole island nations such as the Maldives (see the box at right), could disappear underwater.

Make a KWL chart

Find out more about global warming using library books, news reports, and the Internet. A "KWL chart" will help you organize your research. "K" stands for "What I **k**now." "W" stands for "What I **w**ant to know." "L" stands for "What I **l**earned."

Use the information you have learned in this book to fill in the first column (see the chart below). Questions go in column 2. New facts from your research go in column 3.

What I know	What I want to know	What I learned
Scientists believe temperatures on Earth are increasing.	What are the likely effects of global warming?	

This diagram shows how greenhouse gases work.

3. Most radiation is taken in by Earth and warms it.

2. Some radiation is reflected by Earth and its atmosphere.

4. The warm Earth emits lower energy infrared radiation. Some is absorbed by greenhouse gas molecules. Less heat escapes and so Earth's temperature rises.

1. Radiation from the Sun passes through the atmosphere.

CASE STUDY

Threatened

The Maldives are a group of small islands in the Indian Ocean. No part of the Maldives is more than 2.3 meters (7.5 feet) above sea level. A 1-meter (3.3-foot) sea level rise would put 80 percent of the islands underwater. If global warming continues, the whole nation could be lost to the sea by 2100.

In 2009 the government of the Maldives had a meeting underwater in scuba gear. It did this to bring attention to the dangers the islands are facing.

WORD BANK

atmosphere   layer of gases that surrounds Earth

carbon dioxide   colorless gas in the atmosphere

global warming   rising temperatures worldwide. This is caused by an increase of gases in the atmosphere that trap the Sun's heat.

greenhouse gas   gas in the atmosphere that traps the Sun's heat

Who Produces Pollution and Waste?

Everybody produces some **pollution** and waste. But not all nations contribute equally to these problems. People in **developed countries** produce far more pollution and waste than people in developing countries.

Throwaway society

In wealthy countries such as the United States, homes are full of machines such as vacuum cleaners and dishwashers. Most families have at least one car, computer, and television. Amazingly, people throw away most of the things they buy within just six months. Much of what they throw away is made up of materials such as plastic and metal. These take hundreds of years to **biodegrade**. People also waste a lot of food that they do not eat.

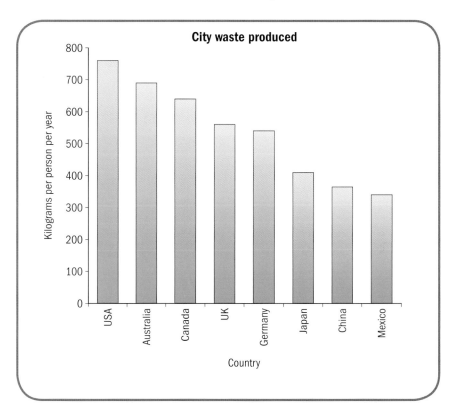

This chart compares the amount of **municipal solid waste** produced per person in cities for selected countries. These numbers are for the year 2000.

High energy use

The machines and gadgets people have in developed countries also use huge amounts of **energy**. People living in wealthy nations represent just 25 percent of the world's people. Yet they use 70 percent of all the energy used worldwide. Most of this energy is created by burning **fossil fuels**. This means that people in developed countries produce far more **carbon dioxide** per person than those in developing countries. So, they are causing **global warming**.

On the bright side, wealthier nations have money to spend on new scientific ideas that reduce pollution (see page 33).

In developed countries, many people regularly eat "fast foods" such as hamburgers and French fries. Fast foods come wrapped in a lot of packaging.

Waste not, want not

In areas such as Africa, parts of Asia, and South America, people have far less money. People often do not own things like televisions, cars, and computers. To save money, people repair vehicles and equipment, rather than throw them away. So, people in **developing countries** create a lot less waste. They also use less **energy**. In addition, a lot more of their waste is **organic** and quickly rots away.

Developing industries

But in the last 20 years, countries such as China, India, and Brazil have quickly become more modern. New factories, **mines**, and **power stations** open regularly. Every week there are more cars on the roads. The number of people in these countries is also rising.

All this means that energy use is rising. So are **pollution** and waste levels. But some developing countries have little money to spend on systems that can reduce pollution. As a result, many areas in the developing world are heavily **polluted**.

Cities in places such as Mumbai, in India, are overcrowded. Poor areas of the city like this cannot deal with **sewage** and waste.

China, an emerging giant

The country of China has expanded its **industries** very rapidly since the 1990s. Its energy needs have grown enormously. Pollution levels have risen, too. Cities such as Beijing suffer from very high levels of air pollution. This has been linked to thousands of deaths a year. In 2006 China overtook the United States as the world's number-one producer of **carbon dioxide**.

In 2007–2008, China opened an average of one new power station per week.

Not in my backyard

Pollution and waste are sometimes caused by **multinational** companies (companies that operate in several countries). These companies set up **mines**, factories, and **oil rigs** in other countries. They take advantage of **natural resources** or cheap costs for workers in other countries. They are sometimes less careful about pollution in other countries than they would be in their own countries.

CASE STUDY

Oil in the Niger Delta

The Niger Delta is an area of land in Nigeria, West Africa, where a river feeds into an ocean. It has very rich supplies of oil. Nigeria has removed oil from there since the 1960s. Oil has also been removed by Shell, a multinational oil company. Oil has made $600 billion in the last 50 years. But it has led to pollution through oil spills and leaks. Many local people use **polluted** water to drink and wash. Local fish supplies have been poisoned. Multinational companies become rich from oil. But local people suffer from very poor living conditions. They are also often in need of jobs.

Soil in the farmland surrounding the Niger Delta is heavily polluted. This makes it difficult to grow food.

The Bhopal disaster

In the 1980s, the U.S. company Union Carbide had a factory near the city of Bhopal, in India. It made **pesticides**, which are substances that kill plant-eating pests. In December of 1984, the factory had a major leak. Poisonous **gases** killed more than 7,000 people. Over 15,000 people have since died as a result of the leak. Union Carbide, now called Dow Chemical, has never properly cleaned the area.

For 25 years, people tried to bring the company to justice. In June 2010, seven local managers were found guilty of causing "death by negligence [carelessness]." They were given a sentence of two years in prison. But the U.S. boss of the company escaped trial.

Many people lost their sight after the poison gas leak in Bhopal.

What would YOU do ?

Should countries pay for all the pollution that happens within their borders? Or should multinational companies that pollute the area pay for the cleanup? If so, how could you make sure this happens?

WORD BANK
multinational   operating in several countries
pesticide   substance put on plants to kill plant-eating pests

Tackling Pollution

Pollution can be dealt with in two main ways. One is to clean up the damage done. The other is to remove or reduce the source of pollution. It is almost always far cheaper to reduce pollution before it spreads. This is also better for the **environment**.

"Polluter pays"

Whenever possible, the company responsible for the pollution must pay for the cleanup. But it is not always easy to get companies to do so. This is especially true in cases of **transboundary pollution**.

Cleaning up oil spills

When a major oil spill occurs at sea, the cleanup effort can cost millions, and even billions, of dollars. Floating barriers are used to contain the oil. The oil may then be skimmed off the surface. If oil washes ashore, hoses and vacuums are used to clean it up. Birds, seals, and other animals covered in oil must be washed individually— but most die anyway. In the long run, it is far cheaper for companies to improve their own pollution controls in the first place.

Make a problem-solving model

This diagram is called a problem-solving model. It is a way to organize facts about difficult issues. The problem box states the problem. Solutions and their results are set out in boxes below. The conclusion box shows what you decide is the best option. Copy and fill in the diagram at right. Use it to summarize facts about acid rain (see page 29).

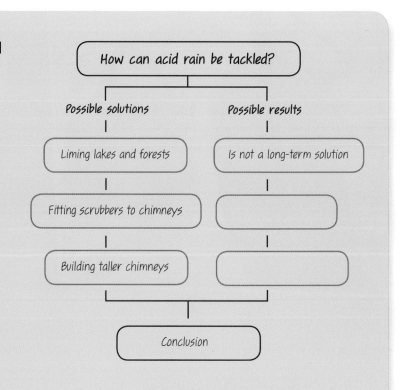

How can acid rain be tackled?

Possible solutions

Liming lakes and forests

Fitting scrubbers to chimneys

Building taller chimneys

Possible results

Is not a long-term solution

Conclusion

Tackling acid rain

The lakes and forests in the country of Japan are **polluted** by **acid rain**. This is caused by the spread of pollution from factories and **power stations** in China. Scientists are trying to solve the problem. Factory chimneys can be made taller. This reduces local pollution. But it does not prevent it from spreading in the wind. Lakes with the harmful substance acid can be treated by dumping a substance called lime on them. But this process is expensive. Its effects are also not permanent.

A better solution is to reduce pollution at the source. Japan is paying for "scrubbers" to be fitted to power stations and factories in China. These clean pollution from the air before it leaves the factory.

A plane dumps lime onto the Sous Dam in the Czech Republic.

Anti-pollution laws

Worldwide efforts to reduce **pollution** took off in the 1970s. Groups such as Greenpeace and Friends of the Earth helped to raise public awareness. The United States and many other countries passed laws to clean up the air, water, and soil. In many countries, government groups were set up to keep track of pollution. They also made sure businesses followed the rules.

Find out more

Environmental protection agencies are government groups that protect the **environment**. Visit your government's website. Type "environmental protection" and the name of your country into a search engine.

Cleaning up cars

The United States, Japan, and most **developed countries** have passed laws to reduce vehicle pollution. Devices called **catalytic converters** are fitted to car exhausts (the pipes that waste **gases** escape from). They capture harmful waste gases, or **emissions**. In many U.S. states, western Europe, Japan, and Australia, car emissions are tested regularly. Vehicles that fail the test are not allowed on the road.

An international agreement called the Law of the Sea Treaty has helped to reduce pollution in the oceans.

Restoring the ozone layer

In 1985 scientists discovered that the **ozone layer** had become much thinner. The ozone layer is a layer of gas high in the **atmosphere**. It blocks the harmful **radiation** in sunlight. These harmful **rays** can trigger skin cancer in humans. The damage to the ozone layer was connected to substances called **chlorofluorocarbons (CFCs)**. These were used as cooling substances in refrigerators. They were also used to make sprays called aerosol sprays, such as hairsprays.

To tackle these sorts of problems, countries have to work together. In 1987 most countries signed an agreement called the Montreal Protocol. It outlawed the use of CFCs. Scientists believe that this measure should help to rebuild the ozone layer by about 2050.

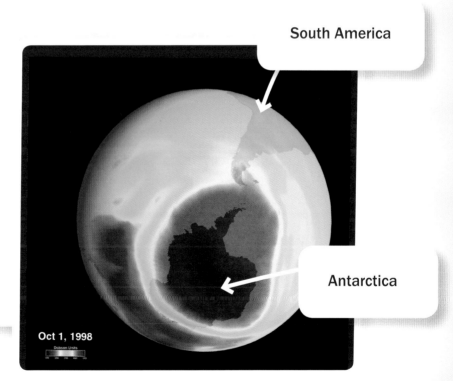

South America

Antarctica

The light purple area on this image shows where the ozone layer is thinnest.

Oct 1, 1998

Dobson Units

WORD BANK

catalytic converter   device fitted to a car exhaust that captures harmful waste gases

emission   release of a gas

ozone layer   layer of gas found in the atmosphere that prevents harmful rays in sunlight from reaching Earth

Tackling climate change

Climate change is a change in the temperature, rainfall, or wind of a region. These changes are brought about by **global warming**. Many scientists believe that climate change is the most serious problem facing our **environment**.

The obvious way to tackle the problem is to reduce levels of **greenhouse gases**. This can be achieved by burning fewer **fossil fuels**. Since the 1990s, the world's nations have tried to reach agreements to reduce greenhouse gases. In 1997 many countries signed the Kyoto Protocol. They pledged to reduce their greenhouse gas **emissions** by 5 percent by 2012. But the United States did not sign. It believed the agreement would harm the country's businesses. A 2009 meeting about climate change failed to reach agreement on further cuts.

This chart shows the world's 10 leading **carbon dioxide** (CO_2) producers in 2006. (Note: Each U.S. citizen produces far more carbon dioxide than each person in China. But China produces more carbon dioxide overall because it has many more people.)

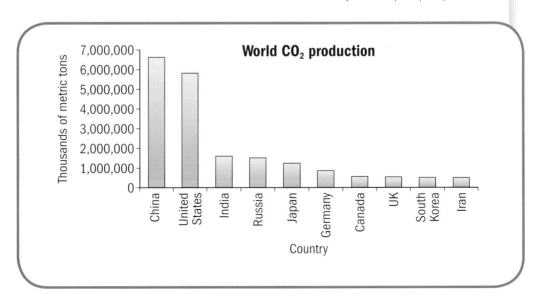

Alternative energies

Burning fossil fuels is the main cause of climate change. So, using different **energy** sources is the best way forward. **Nuclear energy** is one option. But it produces very harmful waste.

Energy sources such as wind power, **solar** (Sun) power, and water power are part of the answer. These forms of energy cause very little **pollution**. They are also **renewable**, meaning they will never run out. But these sources alone do not provide enough energy for the world's needs.

All of these sources have problems, so we will probably need to rely on several options. Beyond finding new energy sources, we simply need to use less energy.

World leaders discuss global warming at a 2009 meeting in Copenhagen, Denmark.

WORD BANK
climate change   change in the regular weather patterns of a region
renewable   fuel or material that can be grown or made again
solar   relating to the Sun

Saving energy

Each and every one of us can help to cut **pollution**. We can do this by using less **energy**. There are hundreds of ways to save energy. Here are a few easy ones:

- Switch off lights when you leave the room.

- Use low-energy lightbulbs.

- Switch off and unplug machines such as computers and televisions. Do not leave them in "standby" mode.

- Make sure your home is lined with materials that prevent heat from escaping. This will save on energy used for heating.

Tackling transportation

Transportation produces about 30 percent of all **greenhouse gas emissions**. The average family car produces more than 4 tonnes (4.4 tons) of **carbon dioxide** a year. You can try to reduce car use by walking, cycling, using the school bus, or using public transportation to get to school. You can also talk to your family about switching to a car that causes less pollution (see the box at right).

Always switch your computer off after you have finished using it!

New fuels for cars

Car companies are developing vehicles that cause less pollution. The Toyota Prius is a **hybrid car**. This mean it runs on gasoline and **electricity** (the flow of energy that powers machines and more). But electric cars still have to be recharged with electricity. This is still mostly created from **fossil fuels**. Cars powered by the Sun are also being developed. In North America and South America, many cars run on **ethanol**. This fuel is made from crops such as sugarcane. But these require a lot of crops. This farmland is needed to grow food to feed people.

In recent years, many cities around the world have introduced cleaner forms of public transportation. The city of New Delhi, India, has ordered the world's largest group of low-**polluting** buses.

WORD BANK
electricity   flow of energy that powers machines, streetlights, and more
ethanol   fuel made from plants such as sugarcane

Reduce, Reuse, and Recycle

The problems of **pollution** and waste can be addressed by the "three Rs" of waste disposal: reduce, reuse, and **recycle**.

Reducing waste

The best solution is to reduce the amount of waste we produce. We can all help to reduce waste by avoiding products with a lot of packaging. You can ask your mail carrier not to deliver "junk mail" like catalogs to your home. In the United States, 100 million trees are used to produce junk mail each year.

Don't use disposable items such as plastic forks and knives and paper plates. If you buy a "fast food" meal, ask the restaurant if it can supply the least amount of packaging possible.

Reusing materials

All sorts of materials can be reused with a little thought. Plastic tubs are very useful as containers. Glass jars can be used as pencil holders. Empty bottles can double as vases or candle-holders. Use both sides of paper before you throw it away. Magazines can be cut up to make cards.

Try to bring a cloth bag with you to the store. That way, you do not need to use plastic bags.

Litter-free city

The city of Singapore, in Southeast Asia, is almost free of litter. This is because there are major penalties for littering. Anyone who drops litter can be required to do 10 hours of community service. The first time someone is caught, he or she can face up to $10,000 or a year in prison—or both. For a second offense, it is up to $20,000 or two years in prison. Most chewing gum is banned because of the mess used gum can make.

Singapore's government puts more limits on individual freedom than some Western countries. It says it does so in order to improve living conditions for all. Do you think other governments should follow this example?

Dropping litter is a serious offense in Singapore. The man wearing a cap is being fined for dropping a cigarette butt on the street.

Economics of recycling

A wide range of materials can now be **recycled**. These include glass, aluminum, steel, paper, and plastic. But the material being recycled has to be fairly valuable to make it worth the cost of recycling. The recycler also has to find a buyer for the recycled material.

Is it cost-effective?

The process of making aluminum is expensive. It also uses a lot of **energy**. Recycling aluminum saves 95 percent of the energy used to make cans from fresh metal. Recycling glass saves 40 percent of the energy used to make fresh glass. Both glass and aluminium can be recycled any number of times without loss of quality.

Paper and plastic are more difficult to recycle. Paper is not very valuable. So, it is hard to make up the costs of recycling. Only a few kinds of plastic can be recycled cheaply. Only 5 percent of plastic waste is recycled.

Glass for recycling is crushed and melted in a furnace.

Waste picking in Asia

In many **developing countries**, people are often very poor. Hundreds of thousands of people, including many children, sort through garbage to find materials that can be sold or reused.

In Bangalore, India, people called waste pickers sort through garbage to find materials that can be reused or resold. They go though around 300 tonnes (330 tons) of waste a day. This work is dirty and smelly, and it can be dangerous.

In the Philippines, in Southeast Asia, around 60,000 people make a living going through waste in dumps outside the city of Manila. In 2000, 300 waste pickers died after heavy rain caused a heap of garbage to collapse. It buried workers' poorly built homes.

Waste pickers sort though waste in a **landfill** site near Bangalore, in India.

Changing attitudes

The "three Rs"—reduce, reuse, **recycle**—are an important part of **sustainable** living. A few years ago, only a few materials could be recycled in countries like the United States. Recycling centers only accepted glass, metal, paper, and fabrics. Many people did not recycle because it took more effort than simply throwing things away. Today, plastics, steel, rubber, old batteries, computers, and cell phones can all be recycled. Easy curbside recycling is more common. Do your part and recycle.

What would YOU do ?

Investigate what is in your garbage can. How much of it could be reused, recycled, or composted?

Buying secondhand clothes is a great way to save money, help the environment—and be stylish!

Sustainable living

Organic materials, such as fruit and vegetable peelings, can be turned into **compost**. Compost is rotting natural material that gardeners use to improve the soil. You can make your own compost heap or find a local compost facility.

You could also try to do a "clear-out" at home. Clothes, toys, and books you do not want can go to a charity store. Or you may be able to sell your items at a garage sale.

Reducing, reusing, and recycling waste help the **environment** in many ways. They preserve **energy** and important materials. They also save on space for **landfill**. The "three Rs" and saving energy can really help to keep Earth safe and beautiful.

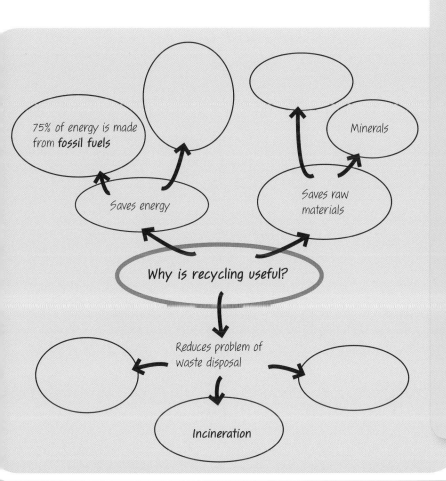

Make a concept web

A concept web can help you organize your ideas and research. Put your main research question in a box near the center. Arrange facts under subheadings. Link them with arrows to the main question. Look at the concept web shown here. It explores the question: "Why is recycling useful?" Copy a diagram like this. Try filling in some of the blank bubbles with information you have learned in this book.

Facts and Figures

World's worst oil spills

1977 A well blows out in the Norwegian Ekofisk oil field. This causes 307 million liters (81 million gallons) of oil to leak into the North Sea.

1978 The wrecked tanker *Amoco Cadiz* spills 258 million liters (68 million gallons) of oil into French waters. It **pollutes** the Brittany coast.

1979 The oil well Ixtoc 1 blows out in the Gulf of Mexico. It spills some 530 million liters (140 million gallons) of **crude oil** (oil in its thick, raw state).

1983 The Nowruz Field platform in the Persian Gulf spills 303 million liters (80 million gallons) of oil.

1983 The Spanish tanker *Castillo de Bellver* catches fire. It spills 295 million liters (78 million gallons) of oil off the South African coast.

1989 The tanker *Exxon Valdez* crashes off the Alaskan coast. It spills more than 38 million liters (10 million gallons) of oil.

1991 During the Persian Gulf War (1990–91), Iraqi troops release 908 million to 1.3 billion liters (240 to 336 million gallons) of crude oil into the Persian Gulf from tankers off Kuwait.

1992 An oil well in Uzbekistan, in Central Asia, spills 333 million liters (88 million gallons) of oil.

2002 The damaged oil tanker *Prestige* sinks off the coast of Spain. It has 76 million liters (20 million gallons) of oil on board.

2005 Over 26.5 million liters (7 million gallons) of oil spill in New Orleans, Louisiana, during Hurricane Katrina. It leaks from pipelines, storage tanks, and factories.

2010 The Deepwater Horizon **oil rig** sinks in the Gulf of Mexico following an explosion that kills 11 people. As much as 60,000 barrels (9.5 million liters, or 2.5 million gallons) of oil per day leak into the Gulf for about three months. This threatens wildlife along the state of Louisiana's coast.

Source: www.infoplease.com/ipa/A0001451.htm

Friends of the Earth's top tips for reducing waste

- Use your curbside recycling program, if you have one.
- Avoid disposable batteries. Use rechargeable ones with **solar**-powered rechargers instead.
- Refuse plastic bags at the store. Carry a reusable bag instead.
- Buy loose fruits and vegetables from a local market or grocer rather than packaged goods from supermarkets.
- Try **composting** your yard and kitchen waste.
- Only print things out from your computer when you really need to. If you do print, use both sides of the paper.

World's smoggiest cities

1. Mexico City, Mexico
2. São Paulo, Brazil
3. Cairo, Egypt
4. New Delhi, India
5. Shanghai, China

Source: www.timeforkids. com/TFK/kids/ns/

Glossary

acid rain rain that has the harmful substance acid in it because of air pollution

atmosphere layer of gases that surrounds Earth

biodegrade rot away naturally

carbon dioxide colorless gas in the atmosphere

catalytic converter device fitted to a car exhaust that captures harmful gases

chlorofluorocarbons (CFCs) substances found in products such as hairspray that damage the ozone layer

climate change change in the regular weather patterns of a region

compost rotting natural materials that can be used to help gardens grow

crude oil oil in its thick, raw state

developed country wealthy country where many people live comfortably

developing country country where many people do not live comfortably

electricity flow of energy that powers machines, streetlights, and more

emission release of a gas

energy ability to do work

environment natural world surrounding us on Earth

ethanol fuel made from plants such as sugarcane

food chain way of describing how living things eat other living things from the level below them

fossil fuel fuel, such as coal, oil, and natural gas, that is made of the remains of plants or animals that lived millions of years ago

gas substance without a definite shape, like air

global warming rising temperatures worldwide. This is caused by an increase of gases in the atmosphere that trap the Sun's heat.

greenhouse gas gas in the atmosphere that traps the Sun's heat

hybrid car car that runs on both gasoline and electricity

incineration when something is burned

industry type of work that creates something to be sold, often through the use of factories and power stations

landfill large pit where garbage is packed down and covered with soil

methane gas produced by rotting garbage

mine area deep within Earth where people dig for substances such as coal

mining removing valuable materials from the ground or deep below the surface

multinational operating in several countries

municipal solid waste (MSW) waste produced by cities, towns, and other settled areas

natural resource something useful that is provided by nature

nuclear energy form of energy that is made by using a metal called uranium

nuclear reactor place where nuclear energy is created

oil rig special equipment used for drilling an oil well

organic made from natural materials

ozone layer layer of gas found in the atmosphere that prevents harmful rays in sunlight from reaching Earth

pesticide substance put on plants to kill plant-eating pests

pollutant substance that harms the air, water, or land

pollute when harmful substances dirty the air, water, or soil

pollution when the natural world is harmed by waste or by any substance that does not belong there

power station place where energy is created

radioactive something that gives off harmful rays of energy

ray line or beam of energy

recycle save garbage so it can be turned into a new product

renewable fuel or material that can be grown or made again

sewage dirty water from homes that contains harmful substances and human waste

smog poisonous, dirty air that forms when polluting gases react with sunlight

solar relating to the Sun

soot black, powdery substance, often resulting from burning fossil fuels, such as coal

sustainable when resources are managed so that they will not run out in the future, causing little damage to the environment

synthetic made by humans, not nature

transboundary pollution pollution that crosses borders between countries

Find Out More

Books

Claybourne, Anna. *Forms of Energy* (*Sci-Hi: Physical Science*). Chicago: Raintree, 2010.

Faust, Daniel R. *Sinister Sludge: Oil Spills and the Environment* (*Jr. Graphic Environmental Dangers*). New York: PowerKids, 2009.

Gorman, Jacqueline Laks. *Fossil Fuels* (*What If We Do Nothing?*). Pleasantville, N.Y.: Gareth Stevens, 2009.

Green, Jen. *Reducing Air Pollution* (*Improving Our Environment*). Milwaukee: Gareth Stevens, 2005.

Simon, Seymour. *Global Warming*. New York: Collins, 2010.

Solway, Andrew. *Environmental Technology* (*New Technology*). Mankato, Minn.: Smart Apple Media, 2009.

Woodward, John. *Climate Change* (*Eyewitness*). New York: Dorling Kindersley, 2008.

Websites

http://kids.niehs.nih.gov/recycle.htm
This website of the National Institute of Environmental Health Sciences offers advice about how young people can reduce, reuse, and recycle.

www.epa.gov/kids/garbage.htm
This website of the U.S. Environmental Protection Agency provides lots of information about garbage and recycling.

www.epa.gov/kids/air.htm
This website of the U.S. Environmental Protection Agency provides facts about air pollution, including links that discuss climate change.

www.eere.energy.gov/kids/
This website, created by the U.S. Department of Energy, offers games, tips, and facts to help young people save energy.

www.greenpeace.org/usa/
Learn more about what the environmental group Greenpeace is doing to protect the environment.

www.foe.org
Learn more about how the environmental group Friends of the Earth is trying to save the environment.

Index

acid rain 18, 28, 29, 31
air pollution 5, 6, 7, 10, 12, 13, 18, 20, 23, 25, 29
aluminum 10, 17, 38
animals 10, 12, 14, 16, 18, 19, 20, 28

biodegradability 10, 23, 24
Brazil 24
British Petroleum (BP) 15

carbon dioxide 20, 23, 25, 32, 33, 34
Chernobyl nuclear power plant 19
China 24, 25, 29, 32
chlorofluorocarbons (CFCs) 31
cleanup 27, 28, 30
climate change 32, 33
coal 6, 7, 10
composting 40, 41

diseases 14, 16, 18
Dow Chemical 27
dumping 5, 14, 16, 26, 39

electricity 10, 24, 33, 35
emissions 30, 32, 33, 34
energy 6, 7, 8, 10, 16, 19, 23, 24, 25, 32, 33, 34, 38, 41
environmental groups 30

factories 6, 12, 13, 14, 18, 20, 24, 25, 26, 27, 29
farming 6, 12, 14, 16, 19, 20, 35
food 8, 12, 16, 22, 23, 35, 36
food chains 12, 14, 15
fossil fuels 7, 10, 19, 20, 23, 32, 33, 35

glass 8, 9, 10, 17, 36, 38, 40
global warming 20, 21, 23, 32, 33
greenhouse gases 20, 32, 33, 34

household waste 8, 16, 17, 22–23, 24, 36
India 24, 27, 39
industry 6, 16, 18, 24, 25, 27
insects 6, 10, 16
international agreements 31, 32

Japan 19, 29, 30

landfills 16, 17, 41
litter 23, 36, 37, 40
local pollution 18, 29

Maldives 20, 21
marine life 14, 15, 18, 26
Mexico City, Mexico 13
mining 16, 24, 26
municipal solid waste (MSW) 8, 9, 22

natural pollution 4, 20
natural resources 8, 17
Niger Delta 26
nuclear energy 7, 19, 33

oceans 5, 12, 14, 15, 20, 33
oil spills 5, 14, 15, 26, 28
organic waste 10, 24, 41
ozone layer 31

packaging 8, 10, 23, 36
paper 8, 9, 10, 17, 36, 37, 38, 40
pesticides 6, 27

Philippines 16, 39
plants 6, 10, 12, 14, 16
plastics 6, 8, 9, 10, 23, 36, 38, 40
"polluter pays" principle 27, 28
power stations 12, 19, 20, 24, 29

radioactive waste 7, 14, 33
recycling 9, 10, 17, 36, 38, 39, 40, 41
reducing 28, 29, 30, 32, 33, 34, 36, 40, 41
renewable resources 33
reusing 36, 39, 40, 41

sea levels 20, 21
sewage 11, 14
Singapore 37
soil pollution 5, 6, 10, 12, 16, 27
solar power 33, 35
"standby mode" 34
sustainability 5, 40, 41

toxic wastes 6, 11, 12, 14, 15, 18, 26, 27
transboundary pollution 18, 28, 31
transportation 10, 13, 34, 35, 38

United Kingdom 19, 30
United States 5, 8, 9, 16, 19, 22–23, 25, 30, 32, 34, 36, 40

water pollution 5, 12, 14, 16, 17, 18, 26, 27, 29
water power 33